maison
CHRISTIAN LIAIGRE

maison

C H R I S T I A N   L I A I G R E

Herbert Ypma

with 550 illustrations, 400 in colour

Thames & Hudson

CONTENTS

INTRODUCTION

I've admired the work of Christian Liaigre for a long time. Yet when he called to suggest the idea of collaborating on a book, I had my doubts. Most monographs, particularly those on interior designers, leave me cold. They are never complete or comprehensive – how can they be if the designer is still alive? The photography is usually sourced from countless different photographers and the text is normally along the lines of 'When I was little I loved blue, and I still do.' Much as I'm a fan of Liaigre's work, I wasn't sure how it could make a compelling book. I was missing the story, and I told him so.

Any other ego would have shown me the door, but Liaigre was open to my position. More surprisingly, he agreed with me. He didn't want a book that was all about him. He didn't even want a book that was all about his work. What he wanted was a book that would really get under the skin of his latest, and in his opinion most interesting, projects – specifically, his domestic projects. He believes in the old adage that there are no great designers, only great clients. The premise was simple: to feature a host of different properties scattered around the world – from a beach house in Galicia to an artist's atelier in Paris to a loft in SoHo to an old farmhouse in Bavaria. The story was of both the similarity and the diversity of these projects; of the way that Liaigre's modern and uncomplicated signature is subtly adjusted and adapted to each specific property and location. It's clear that the clients commissioning a beach house in Spain will not have the same needs as those seeking a family home in Antwerp, or a *pied-à-terre* in Paris for that matter. But many designers would nonetheless impose their will regardless of circumstance. The ability to maintain both consistency and appropriateness is something that really interests me, and so we agreed to proceed.

What neither of us anticipated then was the three-year labour of love our project would become. Organizing photography around the world is a complex business, particularly when the clients are successful, busy people.

Each and every house was specially photographed for the book, and – I might add – in extraordinary detail. Liaigre's work is, to a degree, timeless. It does not rely on the shock of the new to get noticed. His is a design oeuvre that uses sophisticated, yet not always immediately perceptible, changes in texture, colour and shape to create ambience and effect. These were the signature subtleties that we set out to capture.

Finally, a note about the comprehensiveness of this book. It would be great if I could say conclusively that this is the definitive volume on Liaigre's work, or at least his residential work. But it is not. It's a reflection of a particular period in his career. There are projects he has done in the past that are not included and there are projects due to be completed in the near future that are obviously not ready to be photographed. But what counts is consistency. Consistency in all regards – consistency of images, words and layout – to create a finished volume that includes, perhaps most importantly of all, a measure of originality.

HERBERT YPMA

THE LEGACY OF LOUIS XIV

It's not by accident that the French have dominated matters of taste in architecture and interiors – the country's rulers have always insisted on it.

Hordes of people visit Versailles and marvel at the extravagance of it all, but few realize that its splendours were all part of a carefully calculated plan. For the palace was created to act as a commercial example – a monumental showroom, if you like – to promote the nation's industries and crafts. Take the famous Hall of Mirrors. Visitors might imagine this to have been an indulgent folly that catered to the Sun King's not insubstantial vanity. And it's true it suited his taste to stroll from one end to the other catching his own reflection in the light that streamed through the immense windows facing his park. But the sober commercial reality was that its creation coincided with the emerging ability of the French to manufacture 'looking glass' in previously unheard-of dimensions. Until then Venice, with its glass workshops on the island of Murano, was recognized as the world centre of glass-making. But Louis XIV was intent on using his substantial patronage to secure French domination of this and other luxury markets. Thus French glass manufacturing overtook that of the Venetians in both quality and quantity. No one could match French glass-making technology, and international royalty and wealthy bourgeois would make the trip to Versailles to see first-hand the dazzling display that was a direct result of French invention.

Mirrors were just one example of Louis XIV's ambitions for his nation. Clocks, chairs, tables, chandeliers, porcelain, tapestries, silks, velvets, printed cottons: think of something refined and expensive and you can almost guarantee that France dominated not just its manufacture but also its design. The most talented clock-makers were the rock stars of their day – gossiped about, celebrated and indulged, not just financially but with superstar perks such as lodgings in the Louvre in the days that this was still His Highness's Parisian townhouse.

Any nobleman worthy of his blue blood would buy in Paris if he could afford it; if not, he would commission local craftsmen to imitate the style of the French aristocracy. Even when the goods in question were not manufactured in France, such as the Oriental porcelain and silks that were all the rage, the Sun King still insisted that France dominate. The French were among the last European nations to establish a company for trading with the East, but with the King's enthusiastic patronage the Compagnie des Indes was leading the field within a relatively short period of time. And again the French couldn't leave it at that. Textile houses such as those in Nîmes successfully copied and reinterpreted the block-printed cottons from India – 'Les Indiennes' – while Sèvres, the royal porcelain factory, copied and improved upon Chinese porcelain. Even the royal tapestry workshops at Les Gobelins were making woven *tableaux* inspired by the Orient, some of which were given as gifts to the emperor of China.

Thus what can look on the surface like rampant, runaway indulgence was in fact a hugely successful campaign to make France the dominant nation in luxury consumer goods. This was Louis XIV's legacy, and it served as a precedent long after his demise. Perhaps Louis XV and the unfortunate Louis XVI were not so personally engaged with matters of manufacture, but the country nonetheless continued to prosper and lead in all matters concerning style and design. More remarkably France retained this lead despite the ravages wrought by the Revolution. There was a hiccup of course, but the

ascent of Napoleon as the country's self-appointed emperor resulted in renewed dominance. Bonaparte was without doubt a student of Louis XIV, and he soon implemented similar programmes, with the same hands-on involvement. It may seem peculiar to us today, but this great general could be found in his campaign tent on the battlefield flipping through samples of Lyon silk or studying watercolours of proposed furnishing schemes. Napoleon kickstarted the country's devastated industries by ordering as much as he possibly could for his own consumption. In fact, he ordered so much silk from Lyon that until very recently all the ministries in France were still being refurbished with fabrics from his original order.

Even when the balance of power shifted to the British Empire, France never lost its edge in what had by then developed into a proper luxury industry. Its products included Hermès saddles, Christofle silver, Louis Vuitton luggage, Baccarat and Daum crystal, and many many more besides that have since evolved into internationally recognized brands.

France today not only remains dominant in the manufacture and supply of refined luxury goods, but is also one of the few modern nations that has maintained its wealth of craftsmen. The French see no contradiction at all between the high-tech finesse of their TGV train network and the exquisite quality of a hand-stitched saddle. Indeed, in a world where most items are mass-produced, the handmade piece may now be more of a luxury than ever before.

LUXE, CALME, MODERNE

Barely more than ten years ago the accepted signature of the modern interior was white walls and blond timber, a derivative of the Scandinavian formula. Then along came Christian Liaigre with his dark African wenge hardwoods, his bronze hardware and his masculine colour palette of creams, brown and greys. So influential has his style been that it has essentially redefined 'modern'. In hotels, offices and boutiques the world over the combination of dark veneered furniture and cream upholstery has become ubiquitous. If imitation is a measure of success then Christian Liaigre is the most successful designer in the world today. Yet usually it is a case of copying the recipe without regard for the chef or the ingredients. Liaigre's designs are often described as minimal, for example, and if you knew nothing about his work it would be easy to think that. In fact they are only minimal in the sense that an Hermès saddle is minimal, i.e. that almost nothing could be changed or added for them to be improved upon. And like an Hermès saddle, they are also the product of highly specialized and skilled craftsmanship.

The saddle analogy is particularly apt because horses have played a significant role in Liaigre's life and career. Born in the Vendée region on the west coast of France, Liaigre was the son of parents passionately involved in the breeding of horses. He attended the Ecole des Beaux-Arts in Paris and tried life as a painter before returning to the country to work in the family equestrian business. After a few more years he returned to Paris to take up the reigns (excuse the pun) as design director of the furnishings company Nobilis Fontan. Eventually frustrated by their reluctance to showcase his own furniture designs, he decided to set out on his own.

The connection between horses and design may not seem obvious at first, but in fact there is a strong equestrian flavour to Liaigre's work: the leathers, the colours, the attention to detail and the strict privileging

of function over decoration are all qualities it shares
with equestrian culture. The stitching on Liaigre's leather
upholstery is as steady and straight as any you would
find on the finest dressage saddle. And his preferred
shades of chestnut, grey, black and creamy white are
those of stallions and mares.

There's a luxury to his kind of attention to detail that
is both subtle and addictive – like that of an expensive
German car, whose quality creeps up on you slowly but
makes a lasting impression. But, interestingly, when you
talk to Liaigre about his work he doesn't harp on about
the stitching or swoon about texture or stress any of
the qualities you would expect him to wave the flag
about. It's almost as if he takes the quality for granted –
'it's normal, no?' For him the essence of the work is
calm – Zen calm. He's convinced that our incessant daily
exposure to a chaotic onslaught of sensory experiences
creates a need for an environment that induces calm.
The Buddhist parallels are coincidental but clear. Zen
thought likens life to a journey on which each possession
is a burden – the fewer the possessions, the freer we are.
No fuss, no bother, nothing superfluous.

Spend long enough in one of Liaigre's environments and you will find yourself making plans to get rid of stuff in order to reduce your own clutter. And as has happened to many of his clients, you might also find yourself unable to live any other way. Liaigre recalls a pivotal day in his life when it dawned on him that he was in fact living with someone else's taste. The antiques – the family antiques – were pieces from another life. Getting rid of them was like a declaration of independence. For the first time he was free of his father's and grandfather's taste – free to discover himself and understand how he wanted to live.

However great a Liaigre-designed interior may look, it's how it makes you feel that concerns him most. Liaigre is widely acknowledged as a master at creating ambience. What is not so often recognized is his ability to adapt his style to a particular place, inserting a local signature without ever resorting to the obvious or succumbing to cliché. In various projects around the globe he has managed to introduce his distinctive brand of 'luxe, calme, moderne' in a manner that is always uniquely appropriate for its location.

GALICIA, **SPAIN**

GALICIA

One day Christian Liaigre left his studio on rue de Grenelle and stopped to buy some tobacco for his pipe. Someone followed him into the shop. 'Excuse me,' said the stranger. 'You don't know me, but I recognize you – you're Christian Liaigre, aren't you? I thought so. Believe me, I don't normally follow people around but I've kept track of your career from the very beginning and I just wanted to tell you that I love your work. In fact, if I ever have the money, I'm going to get you to design my beach house in Galicia.' They exchanged pleasantries and designer and fan went their separate ways – it's always nice to be appreciated.

Three years later, Liaigre's secretary put a call through to him – 'Excuse me, there's a Xavier Dominguez on the phone. You met each other a few years ago in Paris and he'd like to talk to you.' 'Who?' replied Liaigre. 'Xavier Dominguez. He insists he knows you and must speak to you – he sounds very keen.' 'Hello, Christian. It's me, Xavier. Remember the tobacco shop? I told you if I ever had the money you'd be the first person I would call to design my beach house. Well, I've got the money! When do we start?'

Xavier Dominguez is the brother of Adolfo Dominguez, the Spanish fashion designer. Not everyone has heard of him – his name is certainly not as ubiquitous as Giorgio Armani – but in Spain Adolfo Dominguez is even bigger than Armani. His fashion business operates more than seventy boutiques in Spain alone, and not too long ago, at exactly the right time, the family company went public. Adolfo and his brother were, as they say, 'cashed up'. Hence the phone call to Liaigre.

The Dominguez family has for some time owned a substantial piece of land on an island connected by bridge to the Spanish mainland. It's an idyllic piece of the Atlantic west coast, the stretch north of Porto famed for its mussels. And because the island has long been in private hands it is one of the few places in Galicia that has not been spoiled by rampant development.

BOLD STROKES IN THE **HORIZONTAL** DEFINE THE ARCHITEC-
TURE AND THE INTERIOR OF THE DOMINGUEZ BEACH HOUSE.
THE FIREPLACE IN THE LIVING ROOM – A LONG, **ELEGANT**,
SLATE-LINED RECTANGLE THAT MIMICS THE OPEN FIRES
FOUND IN TRADITIONAL PEASANTS' COTTAGES – IS THE
FOCAL POINT OF AN OTHERWISE UNINTERRUPTED SPACE.
THE DECORATION RELIES INSTEAD ON SUBTLE DIFFERENCES
IN **NATURAL** TEXTURE – DARK COCONUT WOOD, BLOND OAK,
WOVEN SISAL, WHITE LINEN AND THE PATINA OF AN ORIENTAL
RUG GIVE THE ROOM CHARACTER AND BEAUTY.

29

I know this area well, or rather I knew this area well. I grew up here as a child. It was paradise then: the endless deserted beaches and occasional fisherman's shack were straight out of Hemingway's *The Old Man and the Sea*. We lived like gypsies, in a caravan and a tent, and my mother still swears it was the happiest time of her life. Spain was poor then and Galicia was poorer still. However, it was also one of the most historically significant areas of old Spain, with the religious city of Santiago de Compostela as its cultural pearl. Galicia was a seductive mix of blue water and white beaches. The rugged textures and bright sun-blistered colours of the local fishing fleets contrasted beautifully with the exalted imagery and refined architecture of the Catholic churches.

Today Galicia has lost its peasant innocence and the beaches are no longer deserted, but there is still the old ambience – traces of a way of life that is specific to this western stretch of the Spanish coastline. It's an ambience that Liaigre has managed to capture with this house. At first glance it doesn't seem particularly typical of Galicia. The house is large, white, refined and very modern. But look a little closer and you will see that the endless

expanse of the pale slabs of stone that make up the
floor are indeed indigenous to the region. And instead of
curtains or blinds to protect against the blazing summer
sun, the expansive windows feature sliding screens of
woven willow – the same material that fishing baskets
are made from. Not only do these details reflect the local
vernacular but, in Liaigre's capable hands, they amplify it.
The light that is filtered by these screens is nothing short
of sensational. It's the same story in the garden. The
courtyard enclosed by the house features a stepped
series of terraces executed in dark slabs of slate planted
with vivid tufts of verdant wild rice. Sculptural and exotic,
it's certainly visually compelling. But why wild rice?
Again, it's a powerful graphic detail that echoes a local
tradition – wild rice has been grown in this region since
the time of the medieval pilgrimages to Santiago.

Ultimately, however, the most important aspect of the
beach house's design and architecture is how they interact
with the Dominguez lifestyle. This house is completely
in sync with the family's way of living. In the morning,
the whole family turns up for breakfast in white linen and
in the afternoon, after siesta, ecru makes an appearance.

IN THE **DOMINGUEZ BEACH HOUSE**, LIAIGRE'S DISTINCTIVE
DESIGN SIGNATURE IS EVIDENT IN THE ARCHITECTURE, THE
LANDSCAPING AND THE INTERIORS. LIAIGRE HAS ADHERED TO
FRANK LLOYD WRIGHT'S INSISTENCE ON A COMPREHENSIVE
AND CONSISTENT APPROACH BY DOING EVERYTHING HIMSELF.
THE STRONG HORIZONTAL AND VERTICAL LINES INFORM THE
WINDOWS, WALLS, CHAIRS, TABLES, SOFAS AND SWIMMING
POOL. EVEN THE **TREES** OBEY THE **MASTER PLAN.**

THE HOUSE IS LARGE, WHITE, REFINED AND **MODERN**. AT FIRST GLANCE IT DOESN'T SEEM PARTICULARLY TYPICAL OF **GALICIA** BUT LOOK A LITTLE CLOSER AND YOU WILL FIND DETAILS THAT ARE INDEED INDIGENOUS TO THE REGION. TO PROTECT AGAINST THE BLAZING SOUTH ATLANTIC SUN THE LARGE EXPANSIVE WINDOWS FEATURE SLIDING **SCREENS** OF **WOVEN WILLOW** – THE SAME MATERIAL FISHING BASKETS ARE MADE FROM. THE RESULTING FILTERED LIGHT CREATES A POWERFUL GRAPHIC EFFECT THAT RECALLS A LOCAL **VERNACULAR TRADITION**.

In the evening, black linen is the apparel of choice for dinner. First impressions may make you think that this is just too much like a magazine photo-shoot, but the reality is that the house is perfectly suited to the way the Dominguez family like to live. Xavier's wife, Maria, for instance, is an extraordinary cook and her enthusiasm for the culinary traditions of Galicia means that she is often found in the kitchen preparing for the daily family meals. No wonder then that Liaigre was called on to design two kitchens – one for preparation and one for finishing touches. But make no mistake – this is cooking for passion, not for show, because the only audience is the family. There are always brothers, sisters, cousins and friends dropping in for dinner and the table – outside for lunch, inside for dinner – is never normally set for fewer than ten.

Eating, chatting, swimming, reading and sleeping...life is exactly how you would expect it to be in the ultimate summer house. A cynic might reply that all summer vacations are like that, irrespective of the architectural merits of the holiday house. True, but this property captures not only the essence of the perfect summer holiday, but of the perfect *Galician* summer holiday. It's a measure of the extraordinary environment that Liaigre has achieved for the Dominguez family that they rarely these days venture outside of the compound. Moreover, the next house that Xavier and Maria have commissioned Liaigre to work on is their family home, a place stuffed to the brim with heirlooms and the legacies of previous generations – that is, until now.

41

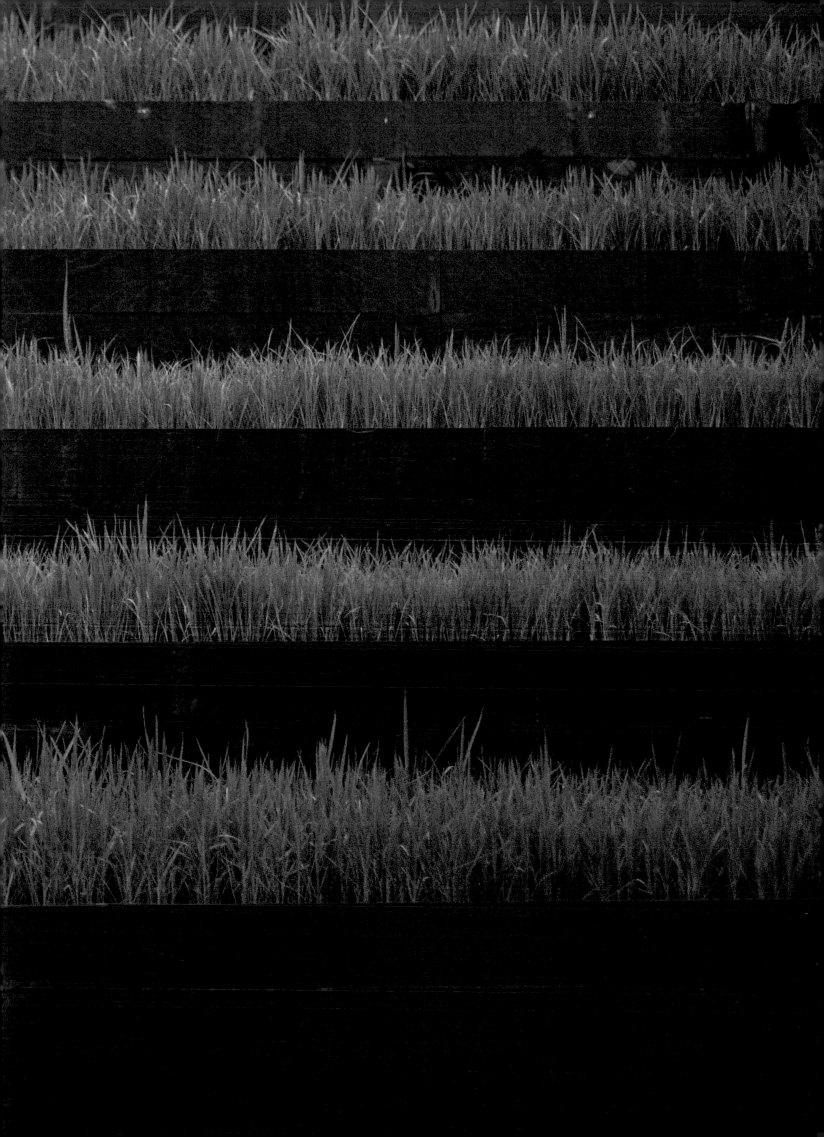

THE SYMPATHETIC AND APPROPRIATE INTERIOR **PALETTE** IS MADE UP OF **SUN-BLEACHED** COLOURS AND RUGGED **NATURAL** TEXTURES. WHITE; ECRU AND THE ODD SPLASH OF PALE BLUE AND BRONZE NOT ONLY REFLECT THE HOUSE'S SURROUNDINGS BUT ALSO ITS OCCUPANTS. IT'S NOT UNUSUAL FOR THE WHOLE FAMILY TO BE DRESSED ENTIRELY IN **WHITE LINEN** IN THE MORNING OR TO APPEAR IN **ECRU LINEN** POST-AFTERNOON SIESTA.

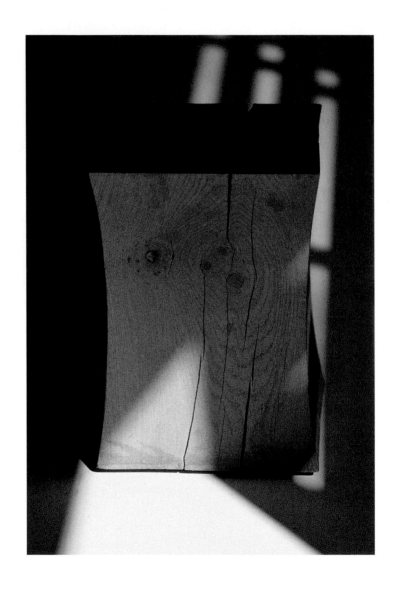

ULTIMATELY, THE MOST IMPORTANT ASPECT OF THE **DESIGN** AND ARCHITECTURE OF THE HOUSE IS ITS SUCCESS IN TERMS OF **LIFESTYLE**. THIS BEACH HOUSE IS ONE HUNDRED PER CENT IN STEP WITH THE WAY THE DOMINGUEZ FAMILY LIKE TO LIVE. THERE ARE ALWAYS BROTHERS, SISTERS, COUSINS AND FRIENDS DROPPING IN FOR LUNCH, AND THE **TABLE** – OUTSIDE FOR LUNCH, INSIDE FOR DINNER – IS NEVER NORMALLY SET FOR FEWER THAN **TEN**.

MONTPARNASSE, **PARIS**

MONTPARNASSE

Picasso, Modigliani, Chagall, Cocteau, Giacometti,
Matisse and Braque – some of the most legendary artists
of the 20th century have been connected with the
Parisian district of Montparnasse. Before the Second
World War this is where they lived and worked. Their
social life centred around the neighbourhood cafes; their
work was pursued in the studios hidden away behind
secluded courtyards and imposing doorways. These days
the art has definitely gone out of Montparnasse – an area
that was once bohemian is now all about shopping.
Yet a few of the artists' ateliers have survived unchanged.
One in particular conjures up visions of an artist toiling
away at a large canvas. The present-day story of this
extraordinary light-filled, double-height studio – the kind
unique to Paris – is about a child raised by his artist
parents in this unusual space. Perhaps in reaction to
his bohemian childhood, Emmanuel Roman grew up to
become an investment banker and ended up living in
London. Nevertheless, as an only child he inherited the
very studio in which he used to live. Although settled in
London, there was no way he could contemplate selling
such a unique legacy and instead he called on Christian
Liaigre to renovate it for use as a Parisian *pied-à-terre*.

The result is intriguing. On the one hand, it looks like
no one has touched it – it is still one hundred per cent
artist's studio, albeit a very handsome one. On the other
hand, it is a thoroughly contemporary space that shows
Liaigre's design skills to their best advantage. The
massive exposed steel beams, the double-storey height
of the main space and the use of books to provide
texture and depth could have been inspired by Pierre
Chareau's famous Maison de Verre of 1932. In a space
of less than one thousand square feet Liaigre has
managed to fit a kitchen-dining area, a master bedroom,
a children's bedroom, a library, a study corner, an
elegant sitting room and a sumptuously spacious and
luxurious bathroom. As an exercise in the efficient
utilization of space, the refurbished atelier rivals a boat.

Every inch has been used without the space feeling at all crowded. If anything, the overall ambience is one of spaciousness.

Despite the client's practical requirements, of which there were many, the *pied-à-terre* has retained the lofty, inspiring look of a studio. Design-wise, the entire space is defined by the double-storey library wall, a robust construction of gunmetal-grey-painted steel beams that provides a point of focus. More importantly, the books are an appropriate contemporary solution to the needs of the present proprietor. Years ago the wall would have been hung top to toe with paintings and drawings, but he is not an artist and the manner in which he chooses to live is naturally different from that of his parents. It's this sensitivity – to the space, to the client and to the location – that sets apart Christian Liaigre's work as a designer. It's interesting, for example, to see his furniture in one of his showrooms, such as the elegant space on the rue du Bac in the 7th arrondissement. You just cannot imagine that these sophisticated, beautifully made chairs and couches would look right in an artist's studio in Montparnasse: too chic and too expensive, you might think. Yet they look completely at home, without creating the impression that the tenant has just won the lottery. Designers universally agree on the importance of this sense of appropriateness, but in this respect Liaigre is the master. Completely saturated with the unique ambience of a Parisian artist's loft, this space is powerfully evocative of its artistic history. Yet there is not a splatter of paint to be seen anywhere.

WITH A NOD TO **PIERRE CHAREAU**'S FAMOUS MAISON DE VERRE, THE DOMINANT DECORATIVE FEATURE OF THIS MONTPARNASSE ARTIST'S STUDIO IS THE BOLDLY STRUCTURAL TWO-STOREY-HIGH **BOOK WALL** FASHIONED FROM **STEEL** BEAMS AND PAINTED AN APPROPRIATELY INDUSTRIAL SHADE OF GUNMETAL GREY.

CHILDREN'S ROOMS WERE PROBABLY NOT A CONSIDER-
ATION WHEN THIS PURPOSE-BUILT **ARTIST'S STUDIO** WAS
BEING DESIGNED IN THE TWENTIES AND THIRTIES. NEVER-
THELESS, A SPACE FOR TWO **KIDS** WAS DEFINITELY PART
OF THE BRIEF WHEN LIAIGRE WAS ASKED TO REVAMP
THE PROPERTY. CLEVERLY, WITHIN A SPACE WHERE ONE
WOULD NORMALLY ONLY CONSIDER PARKING THE VACUUM
CLEANER, HE CREATED A CHARMING ROOM. PART OF ITS
APPEAL COMES FROM THE **VIVID COLOUR** OF HIS SIGNATURE
LILAC LEATHER.

CORSICA, **FRANCE**

CORSICA

Years ago, Corsica was not a place you would consider a suitable location for a newly built vacation house. It was and is beautiful, unspoiled and blessed with magnificent weather, but whatever was built was also in danger of being blown up. Corsica's long-running independence movement had a habit of waiting until a place was finished before blasting it to pieces, and for a while it got so bad that it became almost impossible to insure a building if you were French – or, more accurately, mainland French.

These days, it's no longer a case of real-estate roulette. The violence has abated and the French government has extended certain concessions towards self-government. Corsica is fast being discovered as an alternative to the Côte d'Azur. One of the most popular places to build is the Golfe de Sperone, an idyllic, sheltered, southern corner of the island – not far from the beautifully preserved city of Bonifacio. Facing the Italian coast of Tuscany, it is spared the strong summer winds that buffet the Strait of Bonifacio, but is close enough to benefit from their cooling effect. Sperone is an area with an abundance of sandy beaches and the clear emerald-green waters for which the Mediterranean is famous.

Bomb-wise, however, the new settlers of this vicinity are not taking any chances. The community of Sperone is protected by a twenty-four-hour guard outside a substantial gate and security fencing that defines the perimeter. It's the kind of precaution one would normally identify with Los Angeles, but inappropriate as it may seem, it doesn't really detract from the beauty of the place.

As anyone who knows Paris will tell you, its citizens are strictly divided in their allegiance to places to decamp for the summer. Some swear by the charm of the Ile de Ré, others will only go to Cap Ferrat on the Mediterranean coast, and plenty still subscribe to the glam and glitz of St Tropez. But for a small, select community of Parisians, the Golfe de Sperone is the perfect destination.

They include Alain-Dominique Perrin, whose Golfe
de Sperone summer retreat was designed by Liaigre.
In fact, compound is a more accurate description of
Perrin's property, as it consists of a series of pavilions
interconnected by timber walkways. There is something
part yacht, part Asian resort and part beach cabana
about this simple yet sophisticated arrangement – and,
most importantly, it's not only appropriate for the weather
but also for its location. The predominant feeling
generated by this property is openness. It's almost
as if there are no doors. The only thing that you are
conscious of is the picturesque Golfe de Sperone
everywhere you look.

With floors of polished concrete, bleached outdoor
timber decking and linen slip-covers in ecru and navy,
the interior is an environment perfectly suited to a
barefoot lifestyle. This, for most designers, would have
been enough to define the house – it's definitely a place
that belongs to this particular stretch of Corsica. But
Liaigre, in characteristic fashion, takes things a few steps
further. For instance, the pared-down swimming pool
draws on the tradition of the local stonework and mimics
the dry-stack technique used to build the walls of the

farms and pastures dotted around the countryside. And the colour of the stone echoes the spectacular cliff faces that surround the town of Bonifacio.

The other significant contributor to the ambience – the result, though it's not obvious, of careful design – is the landscaping. The setting of the low-rise, ranch-style compound is cleverly arranged in the same pattern as the surrounding area, with haphazard bushes and odd, tortured trees. The landscaping is as wild as southern Corsica itself. Like the Dominguez's house in Galicia, this summer house is at once thoroughly modern and yet completely of the region. That's the ultimate strength of Liaigre's work. In a subtle fashion he has infused a certain local ambience. Take, for example, the slender timber columns that support the roof of the main pavilion. They are rough, irregular and not perfectly straight, but the timber is dark and beautiful and each pole finishes in a neatly executed series of bases cut from granite. Rough, smooth, dark, light, perfect, imperfect – part of Liaigre's signature is a talent for being able to work successfully with opposites. Corsica has a rugged, untamed nature; so does this house. It is open, unimpeded by walls, doors or windows: raw and pure, like its island setting.

OPEN, FREE AND ALMOST COMPLETELY **WITHOUT WALLS** –
THE SUCCESS OF CHRISTIAN LIAIGRE'S DESIGN FOR THIS
SUMMER HOUSE IS THAT FIRST AND FOREMOST IT INVOKES
THE SIMPLE SPIRITUALITY OF AN **ORIENTAL PAVILION**. YET
THE DETAILING, SUCH AS THE ROUGH-HEWN GRANITE BASES
OF THE SLIM TIMBER COLUMNS, REFLECTS THE INDIGENOUS
MATERIALS AND TEXTURES OF CORSICA.

LONG TIMBER-DECKED **VERANDAS** AND SUN-BLEACHED WICKER FURNITURE ADD A TOUCH OF THE **COLONIAL** TO THE COLLECTION OF PAVILIONS THAT CONSTITUTE PERRIN'S CORSICAN **RETREAT**. BUT THE MOST IMPORTANT DESIGN FEATURE IS THE VIEW – THE **AQUAMARINE WATERS** AND **WHITE BEACHES** OF THE GOLFE DE SPERONE JUST BELOW THE HOUSE PROVIDE A PERMANENTLY SPECTACULAR VISTA.

ANTWERP, **BELGIUM**

ANTWERP

Flat! Ask anyone for the first word that comes to mind when they think of the Low Countries and it is guaranteed to be a reference to how topographically challenged they are. Belgium, it's true, does have mountains, but the area in and around Antwerp is as flat as all of Holland. So it makes perfect sense that some of the greatest contemporary talents in the discipline of garden design have come from this area – because without Mother Nature's indulgence, the only way to add beauty to an unexciting landscape is with the imagination. And so Christian Liaigre ended up working on a project just outside Antwerp with a garden by Belgian designer Jacques Wirtz – one of the most acclaimed creative landscape designers of the past century.

On a plot of land that not too long ago was a cow paddock complete with Frisian cows, a Belgian couple commissioned a house from well-known architect Marc Corbiau and a garden from Monsieur Wirtz. Liaigre was brought in to design the interior. Just like the Dominguez family, this couple had obviously put a lot of thought into their dream house. The result is an unexpectedly modern pavilion that nonetheless retains something of the arrangement and ambience of a Flemish farmhouse.

Once again Liaigre's nose for authenticity led him to focus the interior on the exterior – the spectacular view of Wirtz's work, to be exact. The farm-like flatness of the land is the single factor that defines the Flemishness of the location and that is what inspired Liaigre's scheme for the interior. There is no ornamentation to indicate that the house is in the Low Countries – only the view, which dominates every room. Reflecting Liaigre's penchant for calm, the house's interiors are composed of neutral shades of linen, with tables of wenge and bronze and the odd piece of art-deco furniture, accented with an occasional abstract painting or Thai Buddha. The interior constantly defers to the surrounding landscape.

Architecturally, the house is clearly arranged along the horizontal and the interior design consistently echoes this orientation. The couches, the occasional tables, the footstools, etc, all reinforce the horizontal emphasis. It's not easy to give a modern house in the countryside of Belgium a distinctive Flemish signature without resorting to obvious clichés such as Rubens imagery, black and white tiles and brass chandeliers. A lot of designers have taken this route, but it was never an option for Liaigre, who avoids nostalgia like the plague. Irrespective of location, whether it be Galicia, Bavaria, Paris or New York, he is modern in the pure sense of the word. He works with a visual vocabulary that is largely of his own invention. He is not so arrogant as to create work disconnected from the past; yet neither does he dwell on it. It's a strategy that Liaigre has in common with the giants of modern art and architecture – like Picasso, Frank Lloyd Wright and Henry Moore, he will take what is there, interpret it, reinvent it, but never copy it. Once again the strength of Liaigre's interior lies in his timeless sense of appropriateness.

SITUATED IN THE FLAT LANDSCAPE OF THE **FLEMISH COUNTRYSIDE**, THIS MODERN HOUSE, DESIGNED BY **MARC CORBIAU**, FEATURES A **GARDEN** DESIGNED BY **JACQUES WIRTZ**, ONE OF THE MOST ACCLAIMED LANDSCAPE DESIGNERS OF OUR TIME. ACCORDINGLY THE INTERIOR, A SERIES OF LONG RECTANGULAR SPACES WITH A FLOOR-TO-CEILING EXPANSE OF WINDOWS, MAXIMIZES THE VIEW OF WIRTZ'S CREATION. LIAIGRE'S DESIGN REFLECTS BOTH THE IMPORTANCE OF THE GARDEN AND THE SLIGHTLY MORE SOBER AESTHETIC OF FRANCE'S NORTHERN NEIGHBOUR.

THE **ODD ARTEFACT** OF ANTIQUITY – WHETHER IT BE A MARBLE BUST FROM ROMAN TIMES OR THE HEAD OF A BUDDHA – IS CERTAINLY A PART OF **CHRISTIAN LIAIGRE'S** DISTINCT **AESTHETIC**, BUT IT IS HIS USE AND MANIPULATION OF NATURAL LIGHT THAT CONSTITUTES ONE OF THE MOST SIGNIFICANT STRENGTHS OF HIS DESIGN. **FILTERED LIGHT** IS A QUINTESSENTIAL LIAIGRE SIGNATURE.

LE MARAIS, **PARIS**

LE MARAIS

Together with Ile de la Cité and Ile St Louis, Le Marais is one of the oldest and most historic areas of Paris. Before the Louvre was built, Le Marais was where the king resided – on the Place des Vosges to be exact. As the city centre shifted further to the west Le Marais managed to hang on to its aristocratic traditions, but only just. Eventually it became the city's Jewish quarter and although the odd impressive townhouse could still be found dotted around the area, it was certainly no longer the most desirable address in Paris. By the second half of the 19th century there was so little interest in this quarter that Haussmann's plans completely passed it by. That's why today Le Marais still retains the narrow streets and alleyways that once typified all of Paris. In this respect it resembles much of the 7th arrondissement between Boulevard St Germain and the Seine, but proximity to the government ministries, the Senate and the National Congress has kept real estate prices in the 7th beyond the reach of all but the most well-heeled Parisians.

Not so for Le Marais, which began to be rediscovered by the Parisian artistic community in the late 1970s. Previously disregarded as a ghetto, it slowly became the most fashionable area in Paris. In many ways it still is. Packed with art galleries, interesting boutiques and design-conscious restaurants, Le Marais is now every bit as genteel as the 7th arrondissement on the other side of the Seine. Except for the prices.

Real estate opportunities still arise in this area and one of the most popular is the redevelopment of Le Marais's impressive arsenal of distinguished *hôtels particuliers*. Massive townhouses with impressive doors, courtyards and often a small garden at the back, these mansions are much too large to function as houses but are perfect for converting into apartments. Their extensive cellars are reinvented as underground parking, the courtyards become a green space overlooked by all the residents and the odd ground-floor apartment gets access to the garden.

133

It was exactly such a development that lured Christian Liaigre from the 7th. His previous address in the idyllic surrounds of St Sulpice had been a small pavilion. Charming and unusual, it was also quite dark, so when the opportunity to acquire an apartment with a garden presented itself in Le Marais, he seized it. Apart from the green space that is always at a premium in Paris, the advantages of this property were that the development was still at an early stage, meaning that Liaigre was able to specify his own fixtures, finishes and details.

The most interesting thing about Liaigre's new apartment in Le Marais is that it looks nothing like Le Marais. In the garden you would swear you were in Asia, not Paris. (Bamboo, as it turns out, grows as well in Paris as it does in Jakarta.) Liaigre's approach to gardens is not much different to his approach to interiors. Lack of clutter, simplicity and a sense of calm are the dominant ingredients. It's true that the classic French garden is also simple and free of clutter, but its topiary and gravel spaces were designed to be viewed from a first-floor window rather than to wander through or sit in. A garden on the scale of André le Nôtre's scheme for Versailles is something to marvel at – a miniature version in the city

would be a waste. Instead, what Liaigre has designed for himself is a space to retreat to – a green room that can serve as an outdoor dining area, surrounded by a bamboo curtain for privacy. By combining this with his trademark woven willow screens, he has created what feels like an oriental pavilion without a roof.

A similar aesthetic continues in the interior. The look is indulgent but minimal luxury with an Asian touch. The irony of the design is that it appears almost too perfect to be practical. And therein lies one of the most unusual contradictions in Liaigre's work – because in fact it is always thoroughly based on practicality, even if his refined eye means that it frequently ends up looking anything but practical.

His apartment in Le Marais did, however, present the opportunity for Liaigre to experiment with the interior. The wide-plank oiled-teak floorboards are new, as is the concept underlying the bathroom. Hidden behind a sliding wall, it is possible to sit in the bath while enjoying a view of the living room and the garden beyond. Most importantly, what's clear about this apartment is that Liaigre practises what he preaches and lives what he practises. For it is certainly 'luxe, calme, moderne'.

A **BRONZE TABOURET** BY SCULPTOR ERIC SCHMITT, AN ANTIQUE CHINESE CHAIR AND A VIVID ACRYLIC PAINTING BY TORIE BEGG CONSTITUTE A TYPICAL LIAIGRE COMPOSITION IN HIS OWN APARTMENT ON THE GROUND FLOOR OF A CONVERTED *HOTEL PARTICULIER* IN LE MARAIS. OFTEN INCORRECTLY LABELLED AS MINIMALIST, **LIAIGRE'S STYLE** IS UNCLUTTERED BUT HIS TASTE EMBRACES A COMPLEX APPRECIATION OF TEXTURE, ART AND ORIENTAL DETAILS.

BATHROOMS HAVE BEEN A PARTICULAR CHRISTIAN LIAIGRE
DESIGN STRENGTH EVER SINCE HE CAME TO INTERNATIONAL
PROMINENCE WITH THE HOTEL MONTALEMBERT IN PARIS.
THE COMBINATION OF **DARK WENGE** TIMBER AND **PALE
CARRARA** MARBLE IS BOTH SEDUCTIVELY SIMPLE AND
LUXURIOUSLY DECADENT. THE DOWNSTAIRS BATHROOM IN
HIS OWN LE MARAIS APARTMENT IS NO EXCEPTION. CLEVER
USE OF MIRRORS ADDS TO THE APPEAL OF THE SPACE.
A LARGE SET OF DOORS SLIDE BACK TO REVEAL THE LIVING
ROOM AND ADJACENT GARDEN.

155

DENSITY, DEPTH, DARKNESS: THESE ARE NOT USUALLY
WORDS USED TO DESCRIBE LIAIGRE'S WORK YET THEY
PREVAIL IN HIS INTERIORS JUST AS MUCH AS HIS MORE
FAMILIAR EXPANSES OF PURE WHITE. THERE'S A **NATURAL
CONTRAST** IN HIS WORK BETWEEN AREAS OF **BRIGHT**
LIGHT AND **SUBDUED** LIGHT. THE RECEPTION FOYER ABOVE
IS INTENTIONALLY DIM TO HIGHLIGHT DRAMATICALLY HIS
NEWLY DESIGNED SADDLE STAND. THE WORK TABLE IN
THE LIVING ROOM, DESPITE A FLOOR-TO-CEILING WALL OF
GLASS, IS SHADED BY A GIANT ROW OF GREEN BOX.

TEGERNSEE, **BAVARIA**

TEGERNSEE

Teutonic to the core, the Tegernsee is a handsome lake surrounded by traditional Bavarian architecture and set in densely forested terrain bordered by mountain peaks that stay snow-capped until the end of April. Not far from the Austrian border, the entire area could double as a setting for *The Sound of Music*.

From a distance the place looks rustic, authentic and as though nothing had changed for a good couple of centuries. Up close, you discover that the wooden beam and stucco houses – the kind immortalized by the story of Hansel and Gretel – now contain a lot of expensive avant-garde boutiques.

The Tegernsee is southern Germany's equivalent to the Hamptons. It's *the* escape destination for the worldly citizens of Stuttgart and Munich and is a ritzy, wealthy enclave that has nonetheless managed to maintain the age-old 'gingerbread' look of the Bavarian countryside. But the appeal of the Tegernsee is not just its picturesque appearance, but also what the area offers in terms of activities. In the winter the surrounding mountains provide easy access to skiing and in the summer it's all about swimming, sailing, hiking and cycling.

It's this combination of authentic aesthetic and the great outdoors that drew the Strehles to Bavaria's idyllic alpine setting. Gerd and Gabriele Strehle are, respectively, the proprietor and designer of Strenesse, the pared-down, high-quality German fashion label. Their life is their work – Gerd Strehle's textile company has been in the family for many years – so they really needed a place to relax. Their Tegernsee retreat is a timber farmhouse dating from the 18th century. Apart from its historic integrity, the house also benefits from being no more than one hundred metres from the shores of the lake. It seems ironic today, but in the past a lakeside view was worth nothing; it was the trees that gave the land its value and desirability. A mature fruit tree once made this plot more valuable than the property in front, which is on the lake proper.

The farmhouse may be old but inside there is no mistaking the signature style of a very modern-minded couple. The Strehles involved Liaigre in their project at a much later stage than Xavier Dominguez. They had already commissioned an architect to transform their farmhouse into a weekend home and work was quite far advanced when the question of the light switches began to keep Gabriele Strehle awake at nights. Strehle is a perfectionist and it was her inability to get to grips with this detail that most people would be happy to disregard that prompted the Strehles to contact Liaigre. They had admired his work for some time and specifically loved his minute attention to detail.

Liaigre came on board and, apart from providing an elegant solution to the problem of the light switches, he introduced his particularly seductive sense of 'luxe and calme', but without forgetting about the Bavarian location. Take for instance the oak floor in the barn-like living room (which was indeed previously a barn). Only the keen eye of a true timber aficionado would detect the imperfect hand-planed surface of the planks. And yet this one detail anchors the entire room in the local vernacular. The planks came from a timber yard nearby where the

age of the machinery produced a surface finish that is no longer possible using contemporary equipment. Modern sawmills turn out planks that are too perfect – the finish is so refined that much of the character of the original material is lost. Only in the backwoods of Bavaria can one still find a timber merchant who provides the simpler, more rugged textures of a century ago.

Rugged is an apt word for this house. As might be expected from the credentials of its owners, it certainly has its pristine and polished side, but the aesthetic impact of the interior relies on the contrast between the rough and the smooth. Chunky hand-hewn logs – the kind typically associated with houses in Bavaria – have been used in their original state, and in some instances are stacked to form entire walls. They establish a firm sense of place, creating an ambience that is particular to these surroundings. It's a thoroughly modern house but there is never any mistaking that you are in the midst of the Bavarian Alps. But to describe it as a collection of rough-and-ready old elements juxtaposed with polished new ones would be to do it a disservice. The house gives the overall impression of simplicity whereas in fact, architecturally, it is quite a complex creation.

ON THE OUTSIDE THERE'S NOTHING TO SUGGEST THAT THIS **BAVARIAN FARMHOUSE** IS ANYTHING OTHER THAN A WELL-PRESENTED RELIC. INSIDE IT'S A **MODERN** MARVEL OF SOARING HEIGHT AND DRAMATICALLY INTERSECTING HORIZONTAL AND VERTICAL PLANES WITH A VERY INVENTIVE SPATIAL CONFIGURATION. THE TWO GUEST ROOMS ARE SEPARATED BY A STAIRCASE THAT RISES OUT OF A TRIPLE-STOREY ENTRANCE HALL. LIAIGRE'S FURNITURE DESIGNS SIT ALONGSIDE PIECES SUCH AS THIS CHAIR BY **JEAN PROUVE**.

An example of the careful thought behind this project
is the massive living room. When it was the farm's barn,
the space between the beams was to ensure that the hay
that was stored there would have plenty of ventilation.
Architecturally, it would have been a simple matter to
insert a few more beams into these gaps and then seal
the space, but the Strehles were intent on preserving the
spirit of the building, as well as its character. The design
solution they ultimately opted for was far more expensive
but it preserved these precious three-hundred-year-old
gaps. What they did was to place walls of reinforced
glass behind the beams, thereby preserving the open

appearance but allowing the space to be insulated and heated. The original, massive sliding barn doors were treated in the same manner. They have been left in place, pushed open on the exterior, while on the inside the entire aperture is screened with a monumental slab of glass. Liaigre designed two panels of heavy, quilted leather in roughly the same dimensions that slide along tracts to the inside of the glass to mirror the position of the doors on the outside. There is an uplifting message in this project because it presents an intelligent and stylish lesson in how to both preserve history *and* live a modern life – without compromising either way.

IN GERD AND GABRIELE STREHLE'S HISTORIC BUT IMMACU-
LATE FARMHOUSE THE MODERNITY OF THE **CONCRETE**
WORKS VERY WELL WITH THE RUGGED QUALITY OF THE **OLD**
BEAMS. THIS CONTRAST IN TEXTURE IS CHARACTERISTIC OF
LIAIGRE'S WORK; IT APPEARS AGAIN IN THE LAMPS OPPO-
SITE, DISTINGUISHING THE EXQUISITELY TALL ENTRANCE
HALL, WHICH ARE EXECUTED IN **SILK AND BRONZE**.

ILE DE RE, **FRANCE**

ILE DE RE

Christian Liaigre remembers Ile de Ré from when he was growing up as a child in the Vendée region of western France. It's an area of tough, independent-minded, old-fashioned people with a reputation for dogged stubbornness. This is not an industrial region; people here have always depended on the land and the sea for their livelihood.

For several hundred years, the island of Ré – just off the coast of La Rochelle – was a sought-after piece of terrain because, together with the Camargue in the south, it was a major source of sea salt. The British coveted it for years and the surrounding fortified towns like St Martin are a testament to this. With the advent of refrigeration, salt lost its value and the island reverted to a place filled with sleepy fishing villages enjoying the temperate climate of the Golfe du Morbihan.

Liaigre's childhood memories are of an island untouched by tourism and untainted by the march of modernity. The simple, unpretentious, modest houses of the local fishermen had not changed for centuries – and that's what drew Liaigre back. It may seem strange for someone so attracted to modernity to place so much value on the fact that Ile de Ré has hardly been modernized at all. But Liaigre sees no contradiction in this – he prefers simplicity and authenticity. In fact, when asked what inspires him most in his work, Liaigre has a consistent and simple answer: the sea and the horse. The utilitarian ethos of people who go to sea, whether they are sailors or fishermen, influences his design on many different levels, particularly the materials he favours. Teak and African hardwoods such as wenge, mahogany and sepele have been used as sea-going timbers for hundreds of years, as has the slightly less exotic but equally hardy oak. It's no coincidence that these are Liaigre's favourite ingredients. They may be very chic to some but to a man raised in a no-nonsense region of France they are perfectly rational choices because not only have they stood the test of time, but their looks also improve with age.

In the past, boats also used a lot of bronze, another material which Liaigre has been instrumental in re-introducing to the contemporary lexicon of interior design. The beauty of bronze, aside from its suitability for casting, is its patina. Left outside it will eventually develop a vivid green verdigris. Daily handling, however, will polish the material to a rich golden hue. Thus, like timber and stone, it is a material whose wear and tear adds to its appeal.

Liaigre's work has many times been described as minimal, ultra-modern or pared-down. But I think this misses the point; how can someone who works almost exclusively with exotic timbers, beautiful marble, interesting stone, exquisite silks and linens, wool and bronze be considered minimal? To my mind the word rich is far more appropriate – rich in the old-fashioned sense of impressive yet discreet.

The fishermen's houses of Ile de Ré are interesting not just because they are authentic but also because hardly any face the sea. Villages such as Loix and Arse were built slightly set back from the Atlantic because the last thing any seafaring man wanted to look at

once he got home was the sea. Liaigre has renovated
his fisherman's house in his signature modern manner –
simple, pristine, uncluttered – with not a single cosy
cliché in sight, yet the interior reflects the unique aspects
of Ile de Ré. From the stuffed seagull in the entrance, the
coiled rope hung on pegs in the dining-kitchen area, the
blond woven wicker chairs in the spare bedroom
(recalling the bundles of harvested hay scattered around
the island), to the coral on the mantelpiece, the old
mariners' maps on the walls or the boat oar suspended
above the wardrobes, the house is rich in poignant
detailing and symbolism. And Liaigre has an artist's
feel for authenticity. Even the antique Córdoban leather
screen is the kind of odd valuable object that would
have been passed down in a fisherman's family from
generation to generation. All of it – the interior, the small
patio, the garden – feels honest and authentic. The house
is handsome and sophisticated in a perfectly appropriate
rustic style, yet none of it is predictable. And even more
inspiring, not to mention authentic, is the fact that it
shows the promise of what can be done on a relatively
meagre budget.

191

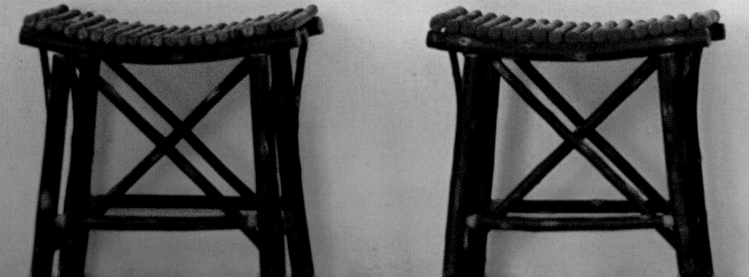

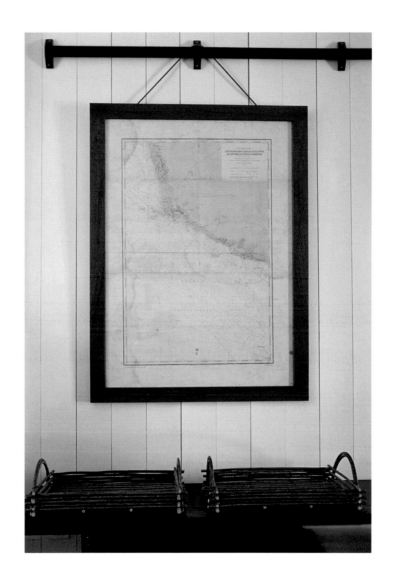

LIAIGRE'S OWN HOUSE ON **ILE DE RE** IS TESTAMENT TO THE FACT THAT HIS SIGNATURE CHIC IS NOT ONLY FOR LARGE SPACES AND BIG BUDGETS. ON AN ISLAND OF **FISHING VILLAGES** AND TINY COTTAGES, AN ULTRA SOPHISTICATED INTERIOR WOULD BE INAPPROPRIATE. YET HIS WENGE WOOD MIRROR FRAMES, LINEN-UPHOLSTERED CHAIRS AND SOFAS, AND FAMOUS TWIG TABOURET ARE COMPLETELY AT HOME IN THIS SIMPLE INFORMAL HOUSE.

UNFINISHED FLOORBOARDS, TRADITIONAL TONGUE-AND-GROOVE WALL PANELLING, INDUSTRIAL-STYLE HANGING LAMPS AND FRAMED **MARINE MAPS** SUSPENDED FROM SIMPLE **BRONZE RAILS** CONSTITUTE THE ESSENTIAL INGREDIENTS OF LIAIGRE'S UNPRETENTIOUS SUMMER HOUSE. IT'S A **FUNCTIONAL AESTHETIC** THAT NONETHE-LESS OOZES A DEFINITE CHIC AND SOPHISTICATION.

SOHO, **NEW YORK**

SOHO

The entrance is classic downtown SoHo – slightly industrial, not at all incompatible with the odd cardboard box lying around. It's not impressive – it was never meant to be – and is certainly not the kind of place you equate with the residence of a media tycoon recently voted the third most influential individual in the world by *Vanity Fair*. Yet for Rupert Murdoch this is home.

SoHo is the only area in all of Manhattan that's skyscraper-free – it was built for warehousing and light industry. The architecture of the buildings reflects their initial purpose – storage. They were designed to maximize open space and in their day were quite advanced structures, with the load placed on slim but weight-bearing cast-iron pillars. Space was the top priority in this area's architectural conception and that's what first attracted the city's artists. Long before loft-living became super fashionable this then rather grubby neighbourhood was attracting painters and sculptors, seduced by the square footage and the affordability of its vast expanses of unencumbered space. For this they put up with the lack of luxuries like central heating and hot water.

A few decades later SoHo has become the most contemporary neighbourhood in New York. The artists, except for the very rich, very successful ones, have long since left, replaced by a posse of photographers, publicists, advertising executives, film-makers, investment bankers, art dealers, and real estate impresarios. Not everyone is happy with this gentrification but it has raised the bar dramatically in terms of lifestyle. High-profile boutiques have replaced low-life pubs and these days most of the inhabitants are dressed top to toe in designer black. It's true that SoHo is nothing like as affordable as it once was and the street cred it once had in the art world has moved elsewhere, but it's undeniable that the place has a lot of life.

It was Rupert Murdoch's son Lachlan who first introduced him to SoHo via the Mercer – André Balazs's groundbreaking loft hotel designed by Christian Liaigre.

Murdoch's divorce from his wife Anna had just been finalized and now that he was a bachelor again the advice from his son was that he should hang at the Mercer just like other high-profile creative New Yorkers. As it happened, Calvin Klein – who was in the process of completing a new home on TriBeCa's West Side – was Murdoch's neighbour on the Mercer's top floor. Then Wendy Deng entered his life and eventually moved in with him at the Mercer. When they got married they started shopping for a new home convinced of two things: it had to be in SoHo and it had to be by Liaigre.

The result is a triplex loft in the absolute centre of SoHo that manages to combine Liaigre's refined sense of 'luxe, calme, moderne' with the open light-filled space for which the buildings of the area are famous. Spread over three floors – four if you count the mezzanine of the enormous outdoor terrace – the dominant theme, design-wise, is space...space and restraint. A lot more could have been squeezed into the available floor area but instead a great deal of care has been taken to maintain the credentials of a loft. For instance, there's only one guest room, although there is enough space for eight.

Both designer and client have respected the integrity of the original dimensions and the history of the area. Where it differs from Liaigre's design work for the Mercer is the Asian element that has been woven into the scheme of things. A touch of China is evident in the wide-planked teak floor throughout the interior, in the dark timber wall panelling of the media room and in the scattering of silk in muted shades of copper and green.

Architecturally, Liaigre has also integrated one of the most distinctive traits of the area – the wooden water towers. Set on the roofs of SoHo like giant rustic sentinels these somewhat crude, gigantic barrels were once the source of water for the buildings. Today most are no longer functional but they are nonetheless protected by the city's preservation code. In most instances the water towers are nothing more than structural icons adding to SoHo's unique visual identity. In Murdoch's loft Liaigre has put one to practical use. In what must surely qualify as one of the most unusual bathrooms anywhere in the world the master bathroom has been built into the Gothic-style cavity directly under the steel superstructure of a large and original water tank.

215

SOHO'S DISTINCTIVE WOODEN **RAINWATER TANKS** ARE NO LONGER USED BUT NEVERTHELESS THEY ARE NOT ALLOWED TO BE REMOVED. THE RATHER SUBSTANTIAL EXAMPLE ON MURDOCH'S EXPANSIVE OUTDOOR TERRACE – COMPLETE WITH BARBECUE – PROVIDED CHRISTIAN LIAIGRE WITH AN INTERESTING DESIGN OPPORTUNITY. HE USED THE **ODD SPACE** CREATED BY THE STEEL SUPERSTRUCTURE UNDER THE WATER TOWER TO CREATE THE **MASTER BATHROOM**.

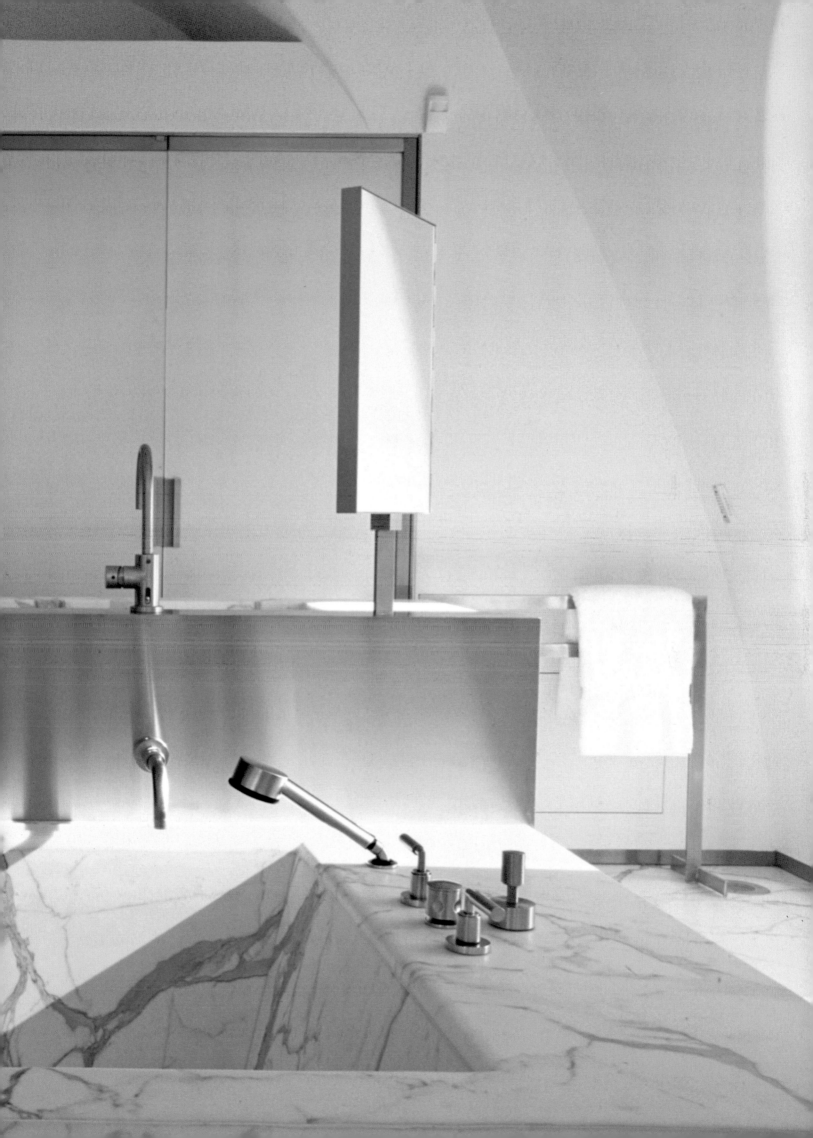

THE EXTERIOR OF THE WATER TANK IS NOT PARTICULARLY PRETTY – IT'S A FUNCTIONAL PIECE OF 'MAKE-DO' DESIGN. INSIDE IT'S A COMPLETELY DIFFERENT STORY: BOTH THE **SPACE** AND THE **DESIGN** ARE TRULY **SPECTACULAR**. THE ORGANIC GOTHIC SHAPE IS STRANGELY REMINISCENT OF SANTIAGO CALATRAVA'S MOST SCULPTURAL WORK AND THE VAST EXPANSES OF SPARSELY VEINED WHITE MARBLE ARE **PURE LUXURY**. BATHED IN SPLENDID LIGHT, THE BATH-ROOM IS MORE LIKE A **MINI CATHEDRAL**.

Inside, this unique space is a pristine expanse of white-
and grey-veined Carrara marble fitted in Liaigre's
signature slabs, once again illustrating how his thinking
about materials goes much deeper than their purely
decorative effect. He uses materials in a manner that
equates as closely as possible with the way that they
are found in nature: these slabs of marble reflect the
proportions of the blocks that are originally quarried in
Italy, just as the wide teak planks on the floor reflect
the dimensions of the tree they came from. Liaigre's
bathroom was thus an opportunity both to explore
something different and to reinforce the ties to the area.

Although completely unlike the Dominguez beach house, Murdoch's loft shares an important quality – the success of the space as a home. It is a living space that is also sympathetic to the needs of Murdoch's creative and working life. In print, TV and film he's obliged to stay abreast, preferably ahead of the game and the loft provides a perfect place to entertain directors, actors, producers, and writers, while the business community, one suspects, would welcome the change from the stuffy Upper East Side. Because there's still a definite artistic credibility that comes with living in this area, despite the inflated prices.

227

STANDING ON THE WALKWAY LEADING TO MURDOCH'S WATER TOWER, **CHRISTIAN LIAIGRE** REALLY IS LIKE THE CAPTAIN OF THE SHIP STEERING HIS DESIGNS IN THE DIRECTION OF HIS CLIENTS' HAPPINESS. AFTER HAVING LIVED AT THE NEARBY MERCER HOTEL FOR QUITE SOME TIME, **RUPERT MURDOCH** WAS CONVINCED OF TWO THINGS – ONE, HE WANTED TO LIVE IN SOHO, TWO, HE WANTED HIS NEW HOME, LIKE THE MERCER, TO BE DESIGNED BY CHRISTIAN LIAIGRE.

COLLECTION

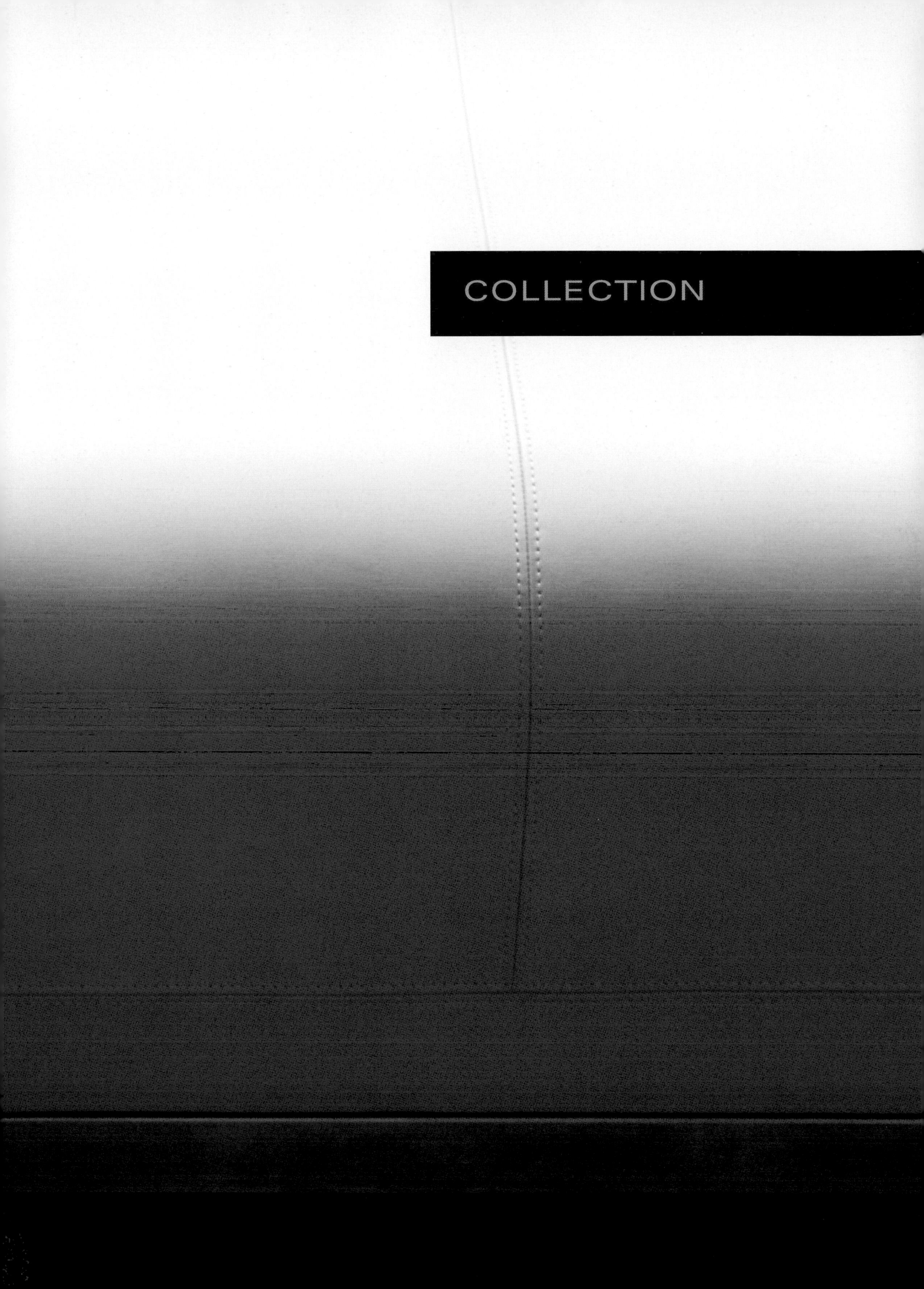

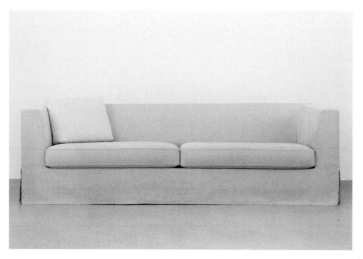

CANAPE ROCCO

CANAPE AUGUSTIN is a very modern, very low, very sexy sofa that appears to float just off the ground. One of Liaigre's most recent designs, it mixes Thai silk with cotton.

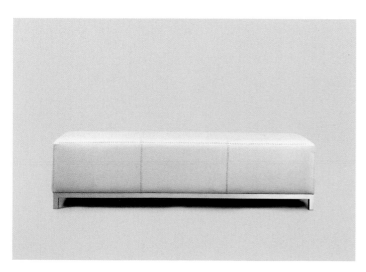

BANC GRUME

CANAPE ROCCO is an evergreen among Liaigre's oeuvre.
Pure, warm and stylishly simple, its slip-cover is made
from Liaigre's own high-quality linen.

CANAPE AUGUSTIN

The GRUME bench, in leather with a brushed-steel base,
is a sleek but practical piece of furniture, providing extra
seating without taking up much space, or obscuring a view.

The ALBUM armchair is one of Liaigre's earliest designs, distinguished by its generous cubic shape and linen slip-covers. It is apparently most popular with men – perhaps on account of its macho dimensions.

ECUME

Reflecting Liaigre's fondness for Asia, CHAUFFEUSE MANDARIN, in leather and stained oak, continues France's centuries-old affair with chinoiserie. Yet, it also breaks with tradition by introducing a very un-French informality.

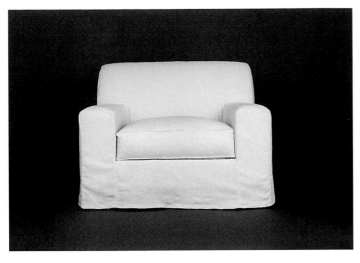

ALBUM

The ECUME armchair is one of the most beautifully crafted
pieces in the collection. Its inspiration is almost pure art deco.

CHAUFFEUSE MANDARIN

FAUTEUIL RE

FAUTEUIL OLON, in stained oak and stitched leather,
is reminiscent of equestrian pursuits. Exactly why is hard
to say, but that's the power of Liaigre's designs – they can
evoke feelings or influences without ever being obvious.

CHAISE VELIN

The FAUTEUIL RE is a sculptural piece of black-stained iroko,
a hardwood from the same family as teak. Evocative of the
sea, its signature design feature is the backrest that recalls
a series of louvres revealing a view of the water.

FAUTEUIL OLON

Tellingly, this is the chair that Liaigre chose for his own
apartment in Le Marais. Much appreciated for its modernity, the
CHAISE VELIN is certainly inspired by art deco, but its master
stroke is the geometric void in the leather-covered backrest.

Inspired by Africa, and made from African wenge timber, TABOURET BAZANE is evocative of a safari in the savannah. In true camping fashion it can double up as a butler's table when a tray is placed on top of the leather seat.

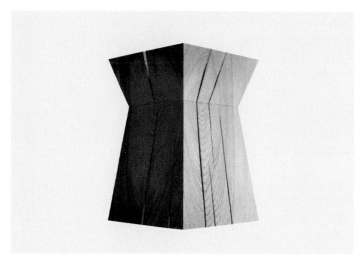

NAGATO

BIBLIOTHEQUE GALET is a melange of inspirations. The organic, pebble-shaped, solid-walnut lozenges (*galets*) that constitute the uprights of this unusual bookcase are both African and maritime in their influence, and the manner in which the space is cut up and divided is very Asian.

TABOURET BAZANE

An homage to Brancusi, the solid-oak NAGATO tabouret
mimics one of the sculptor's favourite shapes. Testament
to Liaigre's love of texture and natural materials is the fact
that Nagato is intended to split. Like many of his designs
it hovers between objet d'art and furniture.

BIBLIOTHEQUE GALET

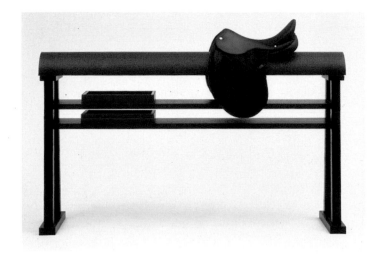

SADDLE BENCH

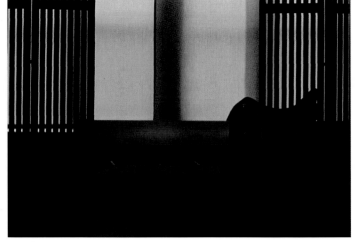

The LAMPE LANTERNE is a traditional Chinese design
reinvented by Liaigre in matt epoxy (for the screen)
and ebonized brass.

BANQUETTE VELIN

The entire oeuvre of Liaigre's furniture is inspired by the sea, the horse and Brancusi. It's only fitting then that he eventually created a SADDLE BENCH specifically designed to display a dressage saddle. As always, there is a practical touch in that the boxes that sit elegantly on the two tiers below the saddle are intended to hold the junk in your pockets (keys, cards, money, etc). In stained oak and leather.

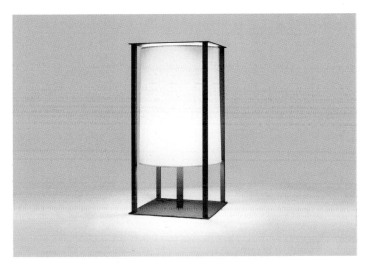

LAMPE LANTERNE

Distinguished by its elegantly refined void, the VELIN series, manufactured in stained oak and leather, is inspired not only by art deco but also by the modern cut-outs of the sixties and seventies: a mix of the bold brutality of Courrèges with the hand-crafted beauty of the art-deco movement.

In Xavier and Maria Dominguez's Galician beach house the
artwork on p. 30 (below right), p. 47 (second from left on
second row) and p. 48 is by Don Freeman; the artwork on p. 36
is by Jean-Baptiste Huynh. In Christian Liaigre's Le Marais
apartment the artwork on p. 137 (below right) and p. 152 (third
from left on third row) is by Peter Beard; the artwork on p. 139,
p. 150 (right) and p. 153 (first from left on top row) is by Torie
Begg; the artwork on p. 150 (top) is by Jacques Martinez; the
artwork on pp. 144-45 is by C. Massimelli; the artwork on p. 22
(top left), p. 136 (below left), p. 151 and p. 153 (first from left
on second row) is by François Nars, the artwork on p. 150 (left)
is by Marc Rebello; the artwork on p. 136 (top left) and p. 147
is by Alessandro Rolandi; the bronze tabouret on p. 139, p. 150
and p. 153 (first from left on top row) is by Eric Schmitt.

First published in the United Kingdom in 2004 by
Thames & Hudson Ltd, 181A High Holborn, London WC1V 7QX

www.thamesandhudson.com

British Library Cataloguing-in-Publication Data
A catalogue record for this book is available
from the British Library

ISBN 0-500-51162-4

Designed by Herbert Ypma and Maggi Smith

Printed and bound in Italy by Conti Tipocolor